Proof of Concept on Utilization of Blockchain Technology in KYC Processes

Dr (Er) Om Prakash

Professor SMS Lucknow

Acknowledgment

I am thankful to the Almighty.
I am also thankful to Professor (Dr) Ashish Bhatnagar
Director SMS, for providing his valuable guidance.

Contents

1

Foreword

This is the industry's first demonstration project of operating Know Your Customer (KYC) procedures using the Distributed Ledger Technology. The project was jointly conducted by SBI Holdings Inc., SBI BITS Co., Ltd. and NEC Corporation with the help of the "Industry-wide Technological Verification in Relation to Blockchain/Distributed Ledger Technology" compiled by Japan Exchange Group. A number of financial institutions participated in this project and were involved in important discussions.

In this project, we first worked out the challenges before newly establishing KYC operation process. Then, we discussed/considered the business process which can solve each challenge in consideration of the law system and summarized the specifications of the prototype system realizing the KYC operation foundation utilizing blockchain technology. After this procedure, SBI BITS and NEC jointly developed an application and conducted verification tests to verify both the technical feasibility and installation effectiveness on business. Finally, we summarized the test results and organized the challenges to be solved for future practical use.

This paper summarizes the details of the newly established business process, the contents and results of the demonstration test, as well as the study of challenges for future practical application. We hope this paper will contribute to early practical use of the KYC operation foundation which can be used and enhance customer services in financial institutions. We also hope it can help to develop the financial services market by receiving various comments from those related to this field, such as those connected to the financial market, and encouraging further discussion.

All opinions and explanations in this paper only belong to the author and do not indicate official statements of Japan Exchange Group, participating companies and organizations to which the author, et al. belong.

2

Current Condition of KYC

Operation of Securities

Companies and Effect on Users

Countermeasures against money laundering or funds for terrorism have recently been an urgent issue in financial markets worldwide.

On the other hand, this trend results in increased costs because financial institutions are forced to continuously take new countermeasures following laws, guidelines or ordinances. The "guideline concerning countermeasures to money laundering and funds for terrorism (draft)[1]" established by the Financial Services Agency in February 2018 is listed as one of the latest guidelines in Japan. This guideline describes the concept of risk management concerning money laundering and funds for terrorism and asks domestic financial institutions to flexibly deal with the change of situation and maintain a risk management system in an effective manner. Under such circumstances, KYC during performing financial transactions is regarded as one of the important measures that financial institutions are required to take. During the process of opening account at a securities company, KYC is also regarded as a very critical operation process and is the subject of this project.

The trend of strengthening restrictions on financial institutions is increasing the procedural burdens while making the process less convenience for users. When opening an account without any face-to-face contact at a financial institution, such as an online securities company, you have to submit a personal identification document that includes picture of your face (for example, driving license), as well as input your personal information including name, address, date of birth and occupation on the website. When you open multiple accounts, similar procedures have to be repeated many times and the number of registration items required for the procedures tends to increase due to the revision of the law system. Under these circumstances, "FinTech Vision [2]," officially announced by the Ministry of Economy, Trade and Industry in May 2017, reported that annually about 1.7 million people among those who want to open an account at a non- face-to-face financial institution gave up opening an account halfway through the process due to the complicated procedures.

---

[1] Reference: "Guideline concerning countermeasures to money laundering and funds for terrorism" issued by the Financial Services Agency in February 6, 2018
<https://www.fsa.go.jp/news/30/20180206/besshi1.pdf> (Last

browsed date: 3.25.2018)

2 "FinTech Vision (report of the conference to discuss the challenges and future direction of FinTech)" issued by the Ministry of Economy, Trade and Industry on May 8, 2017 <http://www.meti.go.jp/press/2017/05/20170508001/20170508001-1.pdf> (Last browsed date: 4.11.2018)

3

Purpose of this project

This project's objective is to make sure that sharing KYC information quickly and securely among securities companies will lead to the enhancement of account opening operation efficiency at securities companies, and also that blockchain technology, which ensures the integrity of data from altering or deleting, can be applied as the system infrastructure.

As mentioned in the previous paragraph, both securities companies and users are now facing the burden concerning account opening operations. Securities companies conduct account opening operation including KYC based on submitted personal information or personal identification documents when receiving the account opening applications from users. This operation is conducted in every securities company. From the cross-sectional view of the securities industry, it can be said that each company partially conducts overlapping operations. On the other hand, users are forced to bear a similar procedural burden every times when opening multiple accounts.

Thus, we believe that sharing the first opening's KYC result when customers open another accounts from the second time on, will reduce the operational burden for securities companies as well as the procedural burden for users who want to open multiple securities accounts. We believe that this can contribute to the enhancement of customer service provided by financial institutions and the development and revitalization of the whole financial services market.

4

Discussion to Establish New Business Process

Aiming to reduce the operational burdens of securities companies and alleviate the procedural burden of users who want to open multiple accounts, we thought the first opening's KYC result should be shared among securities companies at the time of opening the second account or later. However, we acknowledged that there were variations in the details or criteria of the operational process among securities companies. Thus, considering that the commonization of the process is required for sharing of KYC results, we discussed about the necessity of commonization with participating financial

institutions.

– Date	September 8, 2017
– Location	Tokyo Stock Exchange, Inc.
– Participating financial institutions	-Securities companies (on-line)[3] 5 companies -Securities companies (other)[4] 2 companies -Non-securities companies 3 companies 17 members from 10 companies in total

[3] Securities companies mainly provide non-face-to-face transactions using the Internet as a business for individual customers

[4] Securities companies mainly provide channels other than online as business for individual customers

Discussion Results

Based on the discussion results, the project owner continued to consider the sharing of the KYC result. This chapter describes the result, challenges and measures toward sharing them.

4.1. Communization of KYC operation process and installation of consortium

From the reasons described below, we determined that the KYC operation process should be commonized and a "consortium" that will carry out the commonization in a unified manner, should be newly established (Figure 4-2). However, each individual company shall continue to carry out part of the operation process which is difficult to commonize. Details are described in Section 4.2.2.

- Commonization of KYC operation process

Although there are some challenges and concerns which should be solved, we expect many advantages from the commonization, such as unified and efficient implementation of changes when the operation process is revised as well as operation costs reduction through process efficiency. Moreover, by following regulations such as laws and legal acts, it also becomes possible to share the KYC result while assuring a certain level of legal standards.

● Installation of consortium

When there is revision/alteration of laws, the consortium can lead efficient adjustment among participating companies and clarify the location of responsibility. In addition, as operation can be conducted in a unified manner, when compared to the case where each institution individually conducts, we can expect many advantages such as the reduction of maintenance and management costs and operational burdens. Besides, we expect that users who have multiple accounts can change the registration information of all the accounts such as changing their names due to marriage at the same time since their counters are unified.

4.2. Challenges and counter-measures

This section describes the challenges and counter-measures that require consideration when establishing a new business process of installing the consortium.

4.2.1. Challenges and counter-measures in legal regulations

When a new business model is formulated, it becomes clear that there are certain schemes which are not permitted under current laws or that some legal issues require the consideration of counter-measures such as points which need to be organized with a legal interpretation. We discussed these challenges and counter-measures with legal system experts and listed below:

① Challenges

1)　　Omission of personal identification process by sharing identification results at the time of transaction

Fundamentally, the Act on Prevention of Transfer of Criminal Proceeds does not allow the reliance on identification at the time of transaction. However, as an exception, an entrustee can omit the identification at the time of transaction by confirming the identification result of a trustee in the case of a specified transaction entrusted to a specified business operator obligated to conduct identification at the time of transaction. However, the consortium is regarded as an organization only conducting personal identification operation and cannot be a specified business operator obligated to conduct identification at the time of transaction. Therefore, the personal identification process cannot be omitted even when a securities company shares the transaction identification result of the consortium.

2) Utilization of My Number

The "Act on the Use of Numbers to Identify a Specific Individual in the Administrative Procedure ("My Number Act")" does not allow a business operator who has a customer's My Number information to provide the information to any third party even with the consent of the customer. Thus, when a user, who has already opened an account at A Securities Company via a consortium, newly applies to open another account at B Securities Company,

the consortium cannot provide My Number information given by the user to B Securities Company. Thus, the user has to submit My Number again to B Securities Company via the consortium.
3) Declaration of CRS

Based on the "Common Report Standard (CRS), " financial institutions have to confirm the country of the user's residence. This is because any user has to submit the information of financial accounts they have in Japan to the tax authorities of the country in which that user resides. As financial institutions need to receive a "declaration" from users from time to time in order to conduct this confirmation, it is insufficient to only refer the contents of declaration for the initial securities company. It is necessary to receive a customer's declaration again.

② Measures

When consulting with law system intellectuals after identifying the challenges, we received advices that, for Challenge 1), it is necessary to take measures to include companies associated with financial institutions in specified business operators as the consortium is not included in specific business operators under the current laws, and for Challenge 2), it is possible to interpret this explanation as being presented to a securities company on behalf of a user under directions from the user. As a result, we considered measures and established a policy to deal with challenges in legal regulations by separating the consortium organization into the user agent department and securities account opening operation department in this project.

The user agent department conducts the account opening application operation on behalf of users as well as receives all information required to open accounts including specifiable personal information or personal identification documents and also stores the information. It enables users to apply account opening only by asking for a proxy request to the user agent department even for the account opening of the second company or later.

The securities account opening operation department receives the application of account opening from the user agent department and also conducts account opening operation after being entrusted with securities account opening operation (including operation concerning identification at the time of transaction) by each securities company.

4.2.2. Challenges and measures concerning the scope of
        the operation of the consortium

We reached the conclusion that we should carry out operation in a unified manner by commonizing the KYC operation process and should establish a consortium to conduct it. Now, however, there is a process where each company determines whether an account can be opened using its own criteria in the KYC process. Thus, when the consortium carries out the whole KYC operation process in a unified manner, it is required to entrust the determining operation by commonizing even the criteria or letting each company disclose its own criteria to the consortium. Specific challenges and measures are listed as follows:

① Challenges

1) Decision about the result of ASF[5] collation a consortium conducts

In general, a result obtained by ASF collation

only shows whether a collated person belongs to ASF (or may belong to ASF) by checking the criteria or list of collated data. In other words, this result cannot ensure a unique decision about whether account opening is possible. It is necessary to separately make a comprehensive decision based on this result.

2)   Evaluation concerning the principle of ASF collation/compatibility by individual company
Apart from ASF collation conducted by the consortium, there may be a collation process based on the own internal standard of an individual company. Also, each company has its own evaluation criteria or policy about the principle of compatibility based on the "Financial Instruments and Exchange Law[6]."

3) Name identification by individual company
When the consortium conducts name identification for the existing customers of each company, it is necessary to cooperate with the consortium about each company's customer information. Even if it is technically possible to do so, it was said that there are many challenges requiring discussion in other aspects such as the viewpoint of the protection of personal information.

[5] Standing for anti-social forces

[6] Law system for the establishment of rules to protect investors about financial instruments or services

② Counter-measures

As a result of discussions on counter-measures based on the recognition of the above challenges, we determined that the consortium would submit the result of the common KYC operation process to each company and each company would conduct the required process to make own decision same as before. This is because each company's criteria mostly depend on the company's internal conditions and the criteria are treated as confidential information. Therefore, the final decision on whether account opening is possible is made after each individual company's internal process.

5

New Business Process

A new business process was formulated based on previous discussions. For simplification, in this demonstration, users must first apply for new account opening. The range of user properties and application conditions is presented in

6

Overview of Prototype System

In this project, KYC application was developed after building a blockchain platform on Amazon Web Service (AWS). This chapter describes in details three layers of this prototype system: platform (PF), application (AP) and user interface (UI) (Figure 6-1). The contract code of blockchain shall be included in the AP layer and database shall be included in the PF layer.

6.1. Platform (PF)

6.1.1. Types of blockchain

By using blockchain, blockchain participants verify data with each other and record the data with approval. A prototype was designed by the following two patterns calling the structure of participants conducting verification (verifier) as the trust model (Figure 6-2). Notary, appearing in the trust model a, means a verifier providing a signature at the time of transaction and a reliable third party other than the consortium and securities companies.

- Trust model a (Corda v1.0)　　　　: Verifiers consist of "related party + notary"
- Trust model b (Hyperledger Fabric v1.0) :

Verifiers consist of "all participants"

Figure 6-2 Two trust models

While the trust model b is intended to ensure the reliability of data recorded to blockchain by verification conducted among all securities companies participating in blockchain, the trust model a is intended to ensure the reliability of recorded data by verification conducted among the minimum number of verifiers in maximum consideration of the privacy of data.

6.1.2. Network structure

The network structure of the prototype system is shown by each trust model (Figure 6-3, Figure 6-4). The range of PF development is the blank part of each figure. The interface with an existing account system was excluded from the range at the time of the demonstration test.

6.2. Application (AP)

Blockchain data model design

Record of Personal information
Item of Record data
As it is important to ensure the authenticity of
personal information (personal input

information, personal identification document, My
Number document) subject to KYC to ensure the
reliability of the KYC result, record the information
to blockchain.

(1)-2 Record timing

Record information when the new registration of personal information by a user is completed (Figure 6-5 1).

(1)-3 Type of recorded data

Data recorded to blockchain is shared among verifiers. In the trust model b, personal information is hashed and recorded in a way that the person is not identified from the viewpoint of privacy. Personal information not hashed itself is recorded and stored in the personal information database of the consortium. On the other hand, in the trust model a, as only a related party becomes a verifier, personal information itself is recorded in blockchain.

Record the ID of a person in charge of consortium operation, process name, process completion date and time, process result and user ID to ensure the reliability of the person and implementation date and time as well as the KYC results.

(2)-2 Record timing

Fill the KYC results in blockchain every time each process of the consortium is completed (Figure 6-5 2).

(2)-3 Type of recorded data

In the trust model b, the contents of the KYC results which can specify the person will be hashed and recorded to blockchain like the record of personal information.

(1) Record of account opening result

Record the decision result of account opening by a securities company to blockchain (Figure 6-5 3).

6.3. User Interface (UI)

As for the prototype, the UI of a user, person in charge of account opening operation of the consortium and person in charge of a securities company were developed.

7

Demonstration experiments

The developed prototype system was verified from both the technical and installation effect aspects, respectively, in order to make sure that the application of blockchain technology as system infrastructure is possible and the enhancement of the convenience of user's account opening procedures and efficiency of the account opening operation of securities companies can be realized.

7.1. Technical Verification

Aiming for the practical application of a new business process using the developed prototype system, we verified the feasibility from the viewpoint of blockchain technology. In particular, this verification is intended to make sure that blockchain can be applied as the system infrastructure of this business process by paying attention to the difference of a conventional system and blockchain system and conduct verification in consideration of system features inherent in blockchain.

7.1.1. Verification item

The most important feature of the blockchain system is that one system is operated by multiple organizations instead of using any centralized system. Thus, based mainly on this point, we set confidentiality, operability/maintainability, availability and performance/extensibility as verification items referring to the non-functional request evaluation tool of the conventional system "IPA non-functional request grade[7]" and the non-functional request evaluation tool of the blockchain system "Evaluation axis of a system utilizing blockchain technology ver. 1.0[8]."

1 Confidentiality

Separate business process into three classes (Figure 7-1) and verify the following two issues:

The blockchain system, as a single system operated by multiple organizations, will ensure that business processes are carried out with third party auditability and in compliance with rules agreed in advance, as well as the integrity of data recorded to blockchain. Because of this, it is possible to confirm if there is any unauthorized usage, or alteration by the person who perform the business process or the organization operating the blockchain node.

Also, the confidentiality of data is a key point. Thus, confirm that confidential data such as personal information is not shared with any organization other than related parties while the auditability of a third party is ensured by operating one system with multiple structures.

---

[7] Information-technology Promotion Agency (IPA), releasing "non-functional request grade" realizing the visualization and confirmation method of non-functional requests <https://www.ipa.go.jp/sec/softwareengineering/reports/20100416.html> (Last browsed date: 5.28.2018)

[8] Ministry of Economy, Trade and Industry, "Evaluation axis of a system utilizing blockchain technology ver.1.0" <http://www.meti.go.jp/press/2016/03/20170329004/20170329004.html> (Last browsed date: 4.18.2018)

Figure 7-1 Classification of processes in
the verification of confidentiality

1 Operability/maintainability

During operation, in the same manner with the conventional system, we have to assume that the change of business process or modification of an application such as functional improvement may occur. Entailing the suspension of operation of a node like the conventional system at such times is not realistic as the operation of the blockchain node of all organizations in the blockchain system.

In this verification, we verify whether a blockchain application construct code can be updated without system operation being suspended.

1 Availability

For the operation of a system by multiple organizations, the important thing is that the system is normally operated even in the case of the system down or malware infection of a node supporting operation.

For the KYC operation process, the important thing is to avoid the system down of the blockchain node of the consortium to ensure a system where the KYC operation process can be

normally   executed.   Therefore,   in   this
verification, we verify that the service is not

suspended even in the case of system down of the blockchain node operated by the consortium.

1 Performance/extensibility

The blockchain system generally has a low processing speed compared to the conventional system as it processes transactions with consensus building at each scattered node instead of processing in a centralized manner. Thus, it is essential to verify whether required performance requests can be satisfied in order to ensure the feasibility of a business process utilizing blockchain.

In this verification, we verify that the current requests of more than 3,000 account[9] opening applications a day can be processed and the processing performance equal to or more than the number is ensured even when financial institutions operating blockchain nodes are added.

---

[9] Calculated based on statistics officially announced by Japan Securities Dealers Association <http://www.jsda.or.jp/shiryo/toukei/kanjyo/index.html> (Last browsed date: 4.4.2018)

Based on the major items above, we formulated detailed technical verification requests

7.1.2. Verification environment

7.1.2.1. Verification environment of "confidentiality" and "operability/maintainability"

As for each request of "confidentiality" and "operability/maintainability," the trust model a and b were verified under the following verification environment respectively.

With regard to "confidentiality," while personal information is recorded in the ledger of each node in the trust model a, the trust model b is designed to hold it in the DB server of the consortium and record only the hash value of personal information to the blockchain of each node.

1 Trust model a

1 Trust model b

7.1.2.2. Verification environment of "availability"

"Availability" verification is intended to verify that the service is not suspended even in the case of the system down of the blockchain node operated by the consortium. For the trust model a, verification was conducted as a redundant configuration since the blockchain server of the consortium account opening operation department becomes a single point of failure. The verification environment of the trust model b was the same.

7.1.2.3. Verification environment of "performance/extensibility"

In the performance request verification when the number of participating financial institution nodes increases, we conducted verification adding a server one by one when financial institutions are added for both the trust model a and b.

① Trust model a

In the trust model a, every time the number of financial institutions increases by one, the Figure 7-5 system was added to Figure 7-2.

Trust model b

In the trust model b, every time the number of

financial institutions increases by one, the Figure 7-6 system was added to Figure 7-3.

7.1.3. Verification result

1 Confidentiality

The verification result of confidentiality is shown in Table 7-2.

We verified the possibility of alteration detection and sharing range of data for the trust model a and b. As a result, it turned out that data alteration can be detected by another blockchain node by installing the detection function at the application level (Figure 7-7) and personal information is not shared with anyone other than the related party.

1 Operability/maintainability

The verification result of operability/maintainability In order to confirm if the service will be suspended at the time of release of an application (contract code), using the load test tool, we tested the case when the contract code is updated under the state that "new registration of personal information" transactions are being conducted continuously. We verified whether any error that prevent the transaction from being issued would occur continuously.

Result of trust model a: it turned out that, without the update of the contract code at the same time between the related parties of the transaction, the following transaction cannot be issued due to the constraint of this blockchain infrastructure (Corda v1.0 open source ver.). In particular, when the consortium, who is involved with all transactions, updates the contract code ahead of other concerned companies (without adjusting the timing of updates with each securities company), account opening was impossible in each securities company until the update of each securities company.

Result of trust model b: there was no case where a transaction could not be issued because the contract code of all blockchain participants can be updated at the same time due to the function of this blockchain infrastructure (Fabric).

1 Availability

The verification result of availability

In order to confirm if the service will be suspended when there is blockchain node failure, using the load test tool, we tested the case when the blockchain node of the account opening operation department is suspended, under the state that "new registration of personal information" transactions are being conducted continuously. We verified whether any error of "new registration of personal information" would occur continuously before and after the suspension.

Result of trust model a: it turned out that, in the case the node of one of the parties related to a transaction was down, the transaction cannot be issued due to the constraint of this blockchain infrastructure (Corda v1.0 open source ver.). Thus, the redundancy of the node of the consortium related to all transactions is essential. This time, by additionally confirming the feasibility of duplication of the consortium node, we could confirm that the redundancy of the consortium node is possible.

Result of trust model b: the service continued without any continuous transaction error even when system down occurred in any of the blockchain nodes.

However, the system down of the DB server of the consortium which is the registration location of personal information will lead to a transaction error, so its redundancy is essential.

1 Performance/extensibility

The verification result of performance/extensibility is shown in Table 7-5.

We measured the maximum processing performance by gradually increase the multiplicity of "new registration of personal information" using the load test tool. As a result, the processing performance of the trust model a was 3 transactions/second[10] (about 0.25 million/day) and that of the trust model b was 61.7 transactions/second (about 5.33 million/day). This greatly exceeds the current daily number of processed transactions, 3,000.

Furthermore, in order to confirm the influence by the number of blockchain nodes, the existence of processing performance degradation due to an increase in the number of nodes was verified. As a result, in the trust model a, as transactions are shared between only the related parties, performance degradation due to an increase in the number of nodes was not found. In the trust model b, as all participants share transactions, performance degradation due to an increase in the number of nodes was observed.

----

[10] The performance measurement of the trust model depends on
    the result in Corda v1.0 open source version.

    * The conditions of the verification environment are
    described in Section 7.1.2.3.
    * The performance measurement of the trust
      model a depends on the result of Corda v1.0
      open source version. For enterprise version
      measurements, messaging performance has
      improved to 85 TPS.
      <https://www.r3.com/wp-content/uploa
      ds/2018/04/Corda-Performance-ENG.pdf>
      (Last browsed date: 5.8.2018)

----

[11] Number of Securities (number of securities companies),
20 companies, was measured as a reference value of the
"trust model b," where processing performance degradation
was observed.

7.1.4. Study and challenge

Based on the results above, the difference between the trust models a and b is shown in Table 7-6.

T

① Maintenance of contract code

When the blockchain infrastructure (Corda v1.0 open source version) is based on the trust model a, due to functional restrictions, we found that it is necessary to coordinate all organizations regarding the timing of application releases caused by contract code modification and function addition.

One of the features of blockchain system operation is the operation of distributed systems that run blockchain nodes for the consortium or each securities company. However, it is not easy to adjust the release timing among multiple organizations that operate separately. In this case, as a counter-measure for operation failure, we project that the consortium will lead the adjustment of release timing and will release to all nodes in a short time at the same time with the shutdown of account opening. However, this operation should be readily equipped in the release function of the blockchain infrastructure. The presence/absence of the release function can be an important element of the selection of the blockchain infrastructure[12].

[12] This function was added as a function in Cordav 3.0 released since this development
<https://docs.corda.net/contract-upgrade.html> (Last browsed date: 4.4.2018)

② Redundancy of blockchain nodes

We verified the necessity of node redundancy so that as a unified system, the service will not be stopped. In the trust model a, it turned out that it is necessary to make redundant blockchain nodes participating in all transactions like the consortium. This is because the blockchain nodes are divided according to the scope of transaction participants, and nodes participating in all transactions cannot be replaced by other nodes, so redundancy is required. For redundancy, it is necessary to consider the incentive for the costs of the operation organization of the redundant node and operational burden. In the trust model b, as all nodes participate in all transactions, even in the case of any node is down, it can be replaced by other nodes, so redundancy for each node is not needed.

From the viewpoint of sharing recorded data such as personal information, it is basically necessary to make all nodes redundant in the trust model a and redundancy of the external DB is necessary even in the trust model b.

③ Performance impact when blockchain node is added

In the trust model b, as all the blockchain nodes participate in all transactions, the processing performance of the transactions deteriorates as the number of nodes increases. Therefore, it is necessary to set the upper limit of the participating nodes and it is important to conduct a sufficient performance evaluation before starting the service. On the other hand, since the number of nodes included in a transaction is constant in the trust model a, there is no influence on the processing performance through an increase in the number of nodes.

As a result of the above, each of the trust models a and b has its own challenges and additional consideration items, so their pros and cons cannot be generally compared. In particular, as there is a trade-off relationship between a difference in functions between nodes and performance degradation due to a difference in the number of transaction participants, which becomes the cause of (2) and (3) above, it is important to select an optimal model considering the feasibility and costs of solving each issue.

7.2. Verification of results after installation

We verified that when the developed prototype system was put into practical use, whether we could obtain better results compared to the current situation. To verify, we asked the participated financial institutions to try different scenarios using the prototype system and answer the questionnaire and interviews regarding verification items. By doing this, we make sure that the efficiency of securities company's operation at the time of account opening can be improved. Moreover, from the verification results, we also study as much as possible whether the prototype system improved convenience for the users. However, the usability of the user side was not evaluated.

7.2.1. Verification items

In the verification, the following two points were set as verification items. The specific method of verification is described in Section 7.2.2.

Verification item (1) Is it possible to reduce time required by a securities company from application to completion when the account of the second company is opened?

As one of the indicators of operation efficiency improvement, we focused on the time required by a securities company from account opening application to completion. Account opening operation including KYC consists of multiple processes, but some processes are omitted when the account of the second company is opened. Therefore, when opening the account of the second company in this prototype system, we believe that it is possible to reduce the time required to complete the opening compared to the current situation. Therefore, we confirmed whether it is possible to reduce the time and, if possible, how much it can be expected to be reduced by conducting verification. If it is possible to reduce the time from the perspective of the securities company side, even from the viewpoint of the user side, it may be possible to shorten the time taken from application to the completion of opening. Based on the results of this verification, we also discuss this matter.

<u>Verification item (2) Can the operation burden of securities companies related to account opening operation be reduced?</u>

Another indicator for improving operation efficiency is costs and human resources for account opening operation. In other words, if we can expect the reduction of costs and resources by this prototype system for the same account opening operation volume, we believe that operation efficiency can be improved. However, it is difficult to perform a simple quantitative comparison because costs and human resources have various assumptions according to the circumstances of each securities company. Therefore, we decided to verify that the work burden can be reduced instead. This is because the existing work costs and corresponding resources are likely to be reduced if the practical use of this prototype system can mitigate it compared to the current work burden in the company. Therefore, it was confirmed if the work burden in the company is expected to be reduced.

7.2.2. Verification method

For verification, we held a role-play to let participating financial institutions in this project experience a series of account opening processes using the prototype system. We prepared two kinds of cases: "a case where a user applies for the first account opening application" and "a case where a user applies for the second company and later," as a verification scenario and let them experience the cases (Figure 7-10).

After experiencing the role-play, we conducted a questionnaire about this prototype system for the participants and verification by sorting out the results. We also conducted a hearing on the process at the role-play and reviewed verification results based on it to ensure the feasibility of the improvement of operation efficiency from the viewpoint of installation effects.

There was a total of 49 participants in the role-play including personnel in charge of account opening operation.

7.2.3. Verification result

Verification item (1) Is it possible to reduce the time required by a   securities company from application to completion when the account of the second company is opened?

We let financial institutions experience a series of opening operation processes by the prototype system and confirmed whether the time required in the company became shorter compared to before in the case of opening for the first time and opening for the second and later, respectively.

After comprehensively looking at a series of opening operation processes by the prototype system, we asked whether the work burden can be reduced or not. In the questionnaire, we confirmed whether the work burden is reduced compared to the conventional account opening operation at the time of the initial opening and opening of the second company and later, respectively.

Next, we asked how much the amount of work related to account opening can be reduced specifically.

As a result of the hearing, the work volume

undertaken by each company is different, and some companies outsource their work, so it turned out that we cannot simply evaluate the scale of reduction. In the questionnaire, however, more than half of the participants answered that the work volume equivalent to a 2- digit number of persons may be expected to be reduced (Figure 7-13).

Many respondents commented that it is possible to reduce the amount of work in total including outsourcing destinations. On the other hand, some say that it is difficult to judge because the number of account applications fluctuates depending on the time.

7. 2. 4. Study

The study on verification results and contents discussed in a role-play hearing will be described below. The improvement of convenience of the user side will also be discussed in this section although it was not carried out during the verification.

<u>Verification item (1) Is it possible to reduce the time required by a securities company from application to completion when the account of the second company is opened?</u>

From the verification, in the case of the

second company and later, we could obtain the result that the time required to open an account can be reduced. The reason is that, in the process for the second company and later, the opening judgment is made based on the KYC results at the initial opening and a series of processes carried out by the consortium's securities account opening operation department can be omitted. In addition, it was also pointed out that no-forwarding mail can be omitted for residence confirmation.

On the other hand, it was pointed out by multiple respondents that the time required will not change as the necessary process is not omitted as compared with the current situation when an account is opened for the first time. Based on discussions with financial institutions beforehand, the process carried out at the consortium incorporates a process commonly required for each company and is formulated so that the process to be carried out individually on the company side is minimized. Therefore, a counter-measure to reduce time required for initial opening is to reduce the time taken for the operation process itself in the consortium. In the hearing results, from a different point of view, there was a comment that many of the current KYC operations in each company are conducted by hand (for example, visually matching entered personal identification information and information of a personal identification document image displayed on the screen) and it causes mistakes to occur at a certain rate. Therefore, we think that it is possible to shorten the time required for the process itself by automating the matching work, for example, by utilizing OCR (Optical Character Recognition).

<u>Verification item (2) Can the operation burden of securities companies related to account opening operation be reduced?</u>

A majority of securities companies say that the reduction of the work burden in their company is expected by putting this business process into practical use even if the account opening application is the first or later. The reason for this is that the consortium simply carries out the common process on behalf of a securities company; however, some argue that it is possible to reduce human resources taking user correspondence in an irregular case as an example. For example, the response to an inquiry to a user in the case of incompleteness of an identity confirmation document submitted by the user or non-arrival of the mailing item of residence confirmation. Many suggested that the ASF (Anti-Social Forces) inquiry process becomes a heavy burden and there were also many opinions from the viewpoint of reduction of the burden that support the ASF inquiries established at the consortium this time. On the other hand, some argue that individual business processes of each individual company such as its own ASF inquiries remain, so it is difficult to reduce the work burden although it depends on the circumstances of each company. Therefore, for example, we think that there is room for further discussion such as enabling flexible customization, which the consortium deals with according to the circumstances of each company even for the business processes of each individual company.

<u>Enhancement of convenience of the user side</u>

As mentioned in the verification item (1), it was found that the time required for opening an account at the time of the second account opening or later is reduced.

This is because a user does not need to input personal information, upload the image of a personal identification document or receive a no-forwarding mail for residence confirmation, which was essential at the time of initial opening, at the second company and later. In this aspect, as the labor of the user side has been omitted, we believe that convenience has been improved. In this business process, however, as there is still an individual company process such as ASF inquiries unique to a securities company to which account opening is applied, account opening immediately after application is not ensured. When registered information is changed after the initial opening or the validity period of the identity identification document has passed, it will be necessary to conduct KYC again at the consortium. Therefore, it is considered to be necessary for the consortium to consider services that take into consideration the user's convenience by making the consortium notify the user of the presence/absence of

periodic information change or making it possible
for all securities companies to share the changed
information when there is any changed
information.

Other discussion

The freshness and quality of customer information are maintained and enhanced

Financial institutions need to take measures to keep customer information (information on matters confirmed at the time of transaction such as account opening) up-to-date in order to accurately conduct confirmation at the time of transaction following the provisions of the Act on Prevention of Transfer of Criminal Proceeds. In this business process, based on the results of KYC at the time of initial application made by the consortium, a scheme to decide the account opening of the second company and later is adopted. Thus, it is important to be able to maintain and secure the freshness of the user's customer information.

8

Summary

From the verification results, regarding the convenience of the users' account opening procedure and the efficiency of securities companies' account opening operation, we could clarify that a certain level of effects could be expected from the proposed business process. We were also able to demonstrate that blockchain technology could be applied as a system infrastructure to actualize this.

When studying the verification results, we could understand and organize the challenges related to business process operation from both the technical and installation effect aspects. On the other hand, for practical application of the business process itself, it is necessary to prioritize the following themes.

www.ingramcontent.com/pod-product-compliance
Lightning Source LLC
Chambersburg PA
CBHW020503160726
47991CB00007B/2783